YOU CHOOSE BOOKS™

RAPUNZEL

AN INTERACTIVE FAIRY TALE ADVENTURE

by Michele Jakubowski

illustrated by
Federica Frenna

CAPSTONE PRESS
a capstone imprint

You Choose Books are published by Capstone Press,
1710 Roe Crest Drive, North Mankato, Minnesota 56003
www.mycapstone.com

Library of Congress Cataloging-in-Publication Data
Library of Congress Cataloging-in-Publication data is available on the Library of
Congress website.
978-1-5157-8776-1 (library binding)
978-1-5157-8778-5 (paperback)
978-1-5157-8780-8 (eBook PDF)

Editorial Credits
Michelle Hasselius, editor; Lori Bye, designer; Bob Lentz, art director;
Gene Bentdahl, production specialist

Image Credits
Shutterstock: solarbird, background

Printed and bound in the United States of America.
012018   011010R

TABLE OF CONTENTS

ABOUT YOUR ADVENTURE

You feel isolated, miserable, and cut off from the world around you. You see no way out . . . and no way down. That is until a stranger offers you a chance to change your life forever.

In this fairy tale, you control your fate. Let your hair down and make choices to determine what happens next.

Chapter One sets the scene. Then you choose which path to read. Follow the directions at the bottom of the page as you read the stories. The decisions you make will change your outcome. After you finish one path, go back and read the others for new perspectives and more adventures.

A LONELY LIFE

Life can feel pretty lonely sometimes. Even when you are doing the things you love — singing, playing games, maybe even a little gardening — you are all alone. It's as if you are looking out a window high atop a tower. You can see the world below you, but you can't seem to find your place in it.

The people in your life aren't making things any easier. They say they want what's best for you, but you aren't convinced that's true. Sometimes they make you feel downright awful. You dream of a life full of friends and adventure. It's time to spread your wings and leave this dreadful tower. But how?

TO BE ZEL, A HIGH SCHOOL STUDENT READY TO BREAK OUT OF
HER GRANDMOTHER'S PENTHOUSE APARTMENT,
TURN TO PAGE 11.

9

TO BE RAE, A PROFESSIONAL GAMER ON HER WAY TO
SUPER STARDOM,
TURN TO PAGE 43.

TO BE DAME GOTHEL, A MISUNDERSTOOD GARDENER WITH A
WICKED REPUTATION,
TURN TO PAGE 71.

CHAPTER 2

THE IVORY TOWER

"How was school today, Rapunzel?" your grandmother asks. She is the only person who calls you by your full name. You prefer Zel.

"Fine, Grandmother Gothel," you say with a sigh. But it wasn't really fine at all — it was lonely. You don't have a single friend in school.

You and your grandmother live in her penthouse apartment atop a building called the Ivory Tower. It is the tallest building in all of New York City.

11

You understand why your parents sent you here from their farm in the country. The schools are much better. But you don't fit in with any of the kids at school. They dress in dark clothes and let their short, jet-black hair fall over their eyes. You stand out like a sore thumb with your long, blond locks.

To make matters worse, Grandmother won't let you do anything. She insists that you come straight home from school. You've asked her time and time again to let you venture out into the city, but she always says the same thing: "This place has everything you need, Rapunzel. There's no need to leave the tower."

You worry the kids at school think you're a snob because you never hang out with them. You wonder how you'll ever get them to like you.

Then one day things start to look up. After gym class you see a sign taped to the girls' locker room door:

Auditions tonight for this year's school musical.

Open to all students!

A musical, you think. *If I get a part, I'm sure to make some friends.* You love to sing, and you're good at it. Even Grandmother thinks so. Surely she'd let you sing in a school musical. You scribble your name on the sign-up sheet. You have a spring in your step for the rest of the day.

Back at home you head up to your room and open your window wide. As the breeze blows in, you look out at the beautiful skyline. You begin to sing as loud as you can. You feel like the whole city is your audience.

There is a knock on your door, and Grandmother walks in. "Oh, Rapunzel! Your voice is so beautiful," she says.

"Thank you, Grandmother," you reply. "I hope it's good enough for me to get a part in the school musical."

Grandmother frowns. "What's this?" she asks. You start to tell her about the musical, but she starts shaking her head before you can finish.

"No, no, no," Grandmother says. "You are to go to school and come directly home. Those are the rules. You will not be auditioning for any musical!"

TO TRY TO CHANGE GRANDMOTHER'S MIND, GO TO PAGE 15.

TO SNEAK OUT OF THE PENTHOUSE, TURN TO PAGE 18.

14

You feel yourself getting angry, and you ball your hands into fists. "Why can't I try out?" you ask. "It's at school. I'm still allowed to go to *school*, right?"

Grandmother smiles. Maybe there is hope after all. "I'm sorry, dear," she begins, "but school is for learning. A musical is not a good idea."

"Why not?" you protest. You can hear yourself whining, but you don't care. "This isn't fair!"

The smile leaves Grandmother's face. You know what she's going to say. "You have everything you need right here, Rapunzel."

15

TO CONTINUE TO ARGUE,
TURN TO PAGE 16.

TO DISOBEY GRANDMOTHER, AND GO TO THE AUDITION,
TURN TO PAGE 18.

"I have everything I need except for a life," you scream. Grandmother's face turns a scary shade of red. You know you have pushed her too far.

"Rapunzel, apologize right now!" Grandmother demands.

You clamp your mouth shut. You will not apologize. Why should you?

"Well?" Grandmother asks, looking at you with an arched eyebrow. Is it just you, or did the room get darker? And why does Grandmother suddenly look like an evil witch?

When you're sure Grandmother won't hear, you begin to sing. You are almost to the bottom when a door bursts open. Out walks a group of kids from your school.

"It's you!" says Prince, the cutest boy in your grade.

"Um, it is?" you ask, feeling your cheeks warm.

"You're the mystery singer!" Prince exclaims. "Every night I hear singing when I open my window. I could never figure out where it was coming from. Was that you singing just now?"

You nod. "I'm Zel."

"Hi, Zel. I'm Prince," he smiles.

TURN THE PAGE.

A girl you recognize from math class steps toward you. "Hi, I'm Carly. You've got a great voice, Zel!"

"And you've got killer hair!" says a boy from your English class.

You are thrilled that everyone is so nice. One by one they sit down on the stairs, and you all start talking. It feels great to be hanging out with other kids. But wait, what about your audition? You're going to miss it if you don't leave soon.

TO STAY WITH YOUR NEW FRIENDS, GO TO PAGE 21.

TO GO TO THE AUDITION, TURN TO PAGE 24.

You are having a great time with your new friends. You're going to miss your audition, but you only wanted a part in the musical to meet people. Now you have!

After about an hour, Prince turns to you and says, "Hey, the Grimm Brothers are playing at the coffee shop. Do you want to go see them with us?"

The Grimm Brothers is a band made up of two brothers: Jake and Will Grimm. Their music is dark and moody. It doesn't hurt that they are both gorgeous. You absolutely love them.

"Definitely!" you tell Prince. How can you pass up seeing your favorite band? The coffee shop is a few blocks from your apartment building. As you walk you notice that Prince is walking alongside you the entire time. Your heart skips a beat.

When you get there, your group finds a great spot in front of the stage just as the band starts to play. The Grimm Brothers sound amazing! You all dance and sing along. They even play your favorite song, "Let Down Your Hair."

After the concert your group decides to go out for ice cream. You know Grandmother will be heading to bed soon. If you are going to sneak back in, you'd better go home now.

"Mind if I walk you home?" Prince asks shyly.

Wow, new friends and a concert all in one night. It's like a fairy tale! You and your friends make plans to meet tomorrow night. You just hope Grandmother Gothel doesn't find out and ruin your happy ending.

THE END

TO FOLLOW ANOTHER PATH, TURN TO PAGE 9.

You joke around with your new friends for a few minutes. You even tell them about the time you were late for class and started running down the hall. You were moving so quickly that you tripped on your own hair and landed face first on the floor. You smile as everyone laughs.

Then you remember your audition. "I'd better get going," you say nervously.

"Where are you headed?" Prince asks.

"I was thinking about maybe, um, auditioning for the school musical," you say quietly. You worry he'll laugh at you.

"That's a great idea!" Prince says. "With that voice, you'll get a part for sure."

"Thanks!" you reply. You have such a big smile on your face that it hurts your cheeks.

You say goodbye to your new friends and head down the stairs. After a few minutes, you hear someone running down the steps behind you. You turn to see Prince.

"Hey!" he says, pausing to catch his breath. "I was thinking about auditioning too. Do you mind if I go with you?"

"That'd be great!" you tell him.

Prince looks at his watch. "The auditions aren't for another hour. Do you want to leave now or meet in a little while?"

25

TO WAIT,
TURN TO PAGE 26.

TO GO TO THE AUDITION EARLY,
TURN TO PAGE 35.

You don't want to get to the audition too early. You might get nervous and chicken out while you're waiting. You decide to meet Prince later. He walks you back upstairs to your apartment. You talk and laugh the whole way.

"See you soon," Prince says and heads back down the stairs.

It's too risky to sneak back into your apartment, so you wait at the end of the hallway. You think about Prince and your other new friends. You're so happy you start to sing. Suddenly your apartment door flies open.

"Where have you been?" Grandmother booms. She is standing with her arms crossed over her chest. Her face is a frightening shade of red. "And who was that boy?"

"B-b-boy? What boy?" you stammer.

"I came into the kitchen and heard voices in the stairwell," Grandmother says. "When I looked out the peephole, I saw you talking to a strange boy. How dare you sneak out of this apartment! Tell me what is going on this instant!"

TO TELL GRANDMOTHER THE TRUTH,
TURN TO PAGE 28.

TO MAKE UP A STORY,
TURN TO PAGE 32.

You are so flustered. You've never seen your grandmother so mad. You swear you see smoke coming out of her ears.

"Well?" she demands.

You decide to tell the truth. "I was singing in the stairwell and met some kids from school," you say. "I haven't made any friends since moving here. For once I felt like I fit in." Your voice begins to crack as a tear rolls down your cheek.

Your grandmother doesn't say anything. Is she moved by your story? Does she finally understand how you feel? Before you can find out, you both hear singing coming from the stairwell.

"Rapunzel, Rapunzel! Let down your long hair!" Prince is outside the door singing your favorite Grimm Brothers song.

A fresh wave of fury crosses Grandmother's face, and she throws her arms up in frustration.

"I've had enough, Rapunzel," Grandmother says. "Why do you want to fit in when you can stand out? I'm tired of fighting with you. If you want short hair, you can have it."

"Really?" you ask happily. You both head to the bathroom, and Grandmother begins to cut your hair. Soon blond strands of hair litter the bathroom floor. When your haircut is finished, you both look in the mirror.

"At least now that boy has nothing to sing about," Grandmother mutters under her breath. "His voice was terrible."

29

TURN THE PAGE.

30

The next day at school, you feel the back of your hair as you walk down the hallway. Your grandmother gave you a short, asymmetrical hairstyle. You're excited to see what your friends think. You see Prince by the lockers.

"Wow! Cool hair, Zel!" Prince says.

Carly walks up behind him. "Yeah, your hair looks great," she says. "We should all hang out again this weekend."

"Sure," you say confidently. "I just have to ask my—"

Then you remember your punishment for sneaking out. *This is just great,* you think. *I have new friends, a great hairstyle, and I'm grounded. Grandmother will never let me leave the Ivory Tower again!*

31

THE END
TO FOLLOW ANOTHER PATH, TURN TO PAGE 9.

"Well?" Grandmother demands furiously. "What is going on?"

"Well, you see," you begin, "I was upset about the musical and—"

"Not that again!" she interrupts. "I said no!"

"I know!" you tell her. "But I heard that . . . um . . . exercise can help calm you down. I decided to jog up and down the stairs. It worked! I feel much calmer now."

Grandmother narrows her eyes. "Then who was the boy I heard?"

"Oh, him?" you say with a wave of your hand. "I have no idea. He was taking out the trash, I think."

Your grandmother frowns, but she doesn't say anything. Does she believe your story?

"We can discuss this later," she says. "For now go to your room."

Relieved, you head toward your room. You are almost there when you hear a light knock on the kitchen door. Your heart sinks.

"Zel? You there?" you hear Prince call.

Your grandmother must have opened the door, because you hear Prince more clearly. "Hello. You must be Zel's grandmother. I'm—"

"I don't care who you are!" your grandmother barks. "You are never to come back here! Do you understand? Now head back down those stairs before I push you down!"

33

TURN THE PAGE.

Grandmother slams the door and spins around as you enter the kitchen. "And you, my dear, are headed back to your parents' farm!"

You are surprised to find yourself smiling. You hadn't realized how much you've missed your parents, friends, and life on the farm. You've been trying so hard to fit in here that you forgot there was a place where you've always belonged. You can't want to leave the Ivory Tower and go home!

THE END

TO FOLLOW ANOTHER PATH, TURN TO PAGE 9.

You better not sneak in and out again. You decide to leave now. You finish your trek down the stairs and out of the building. It takes a while, but you and Prince find a cab. You are laughing and having fun when suddenly the cab comes to a stop. You look up to see a massive traffic jam ahead of you.

"This traffic looks pretty bad," Prince says. "What do you want to do?"

On a whim you say, "Let's make a run for it!"

Prince quickly pays the cab driver. You both jump out of the cab and start running. Prince knows a shortcut, and you arrive at the school without a second to spare.

35

TURN THE PAGE.

"Just in time!" says Mrs. Vargo, the drama teacher. She sets the sign-up sheet down on the table. "Are you two trying out for the musical?"

Out of breath, you and Prince nod your heads. "Wonderful," says Mrs. Vargo. "Will you be singing a solo or duet?"

36

TO TRY OUT AS A DUET,
GO TO PAGE 37.

TO SING A SOLO,
TURN TO PAGE 40.

"A duet!" you both say at the same time. You look at each other and laugh. You hadn't planned on singing together, but it seems like a good idea.

"Great," Mrs. Vargo smiles. "Everyone else is singing individually, so why don't you go first?"

As you walk onto the stage, you see a stand with song lyrics. It's from a Grimm Brothers song — what luck! You are a big fan and already know the words by heart. But Prince is studying them intently.

The song starts and you sing your part well. Then it's Prince's turn. He belts out, "Let down your hair!"

37

TURN THE PAGE.

Suddenly the lights lower, and a spotlight shines brightly on you and Prince. You don't mind the light, but Prince puts his hands up to his face and covers his eyes.

"My eyes!" he whispers. "I can't see anything." His eyes water as he tries to sing the rest of the song. He can't see the lyrics and struggles. Plus he is not a very good singer.

When the song is over, there is light clapping from the audience as the lights go up. There's no way either one of you is getting a part in the school musical after a performance like that.

As you exit the stage, Prince lowers his head and rubs his eyes. "I guess I should have told you that I can't sing very well."

Shocked you ask, "Why did you want to audition with me if you can't sing?"

Prince shrugs. "I thought you needed help. You looked so nervous before. I thought it would be easier if you auditioned with a friend."

You sigh. "It was a nice thought, Prince. But ask me next time. I didn't need to be rescued."

THE END

TO FOLLOW ANOTHER PATH, TURN TO PAGE 9.

"Solo," Prince says immediately. "I've heard her sing, and there is no way I can keep up!"

"Name and song, please," Mrs. Vargo says. You're starting to get nervous. You struggle to say your name before telling her the song.

As she jots it down on her clipboard, Mrs. Vargo says, "Rapunzel, Rapunzel, Let Down Your Hair — got it!"

When it's your turn, you step out onstage and close your eyes. You imagine yourself high up in your room singing out of your window. When the song is finished, you open your eyes and see the crowd on their feet. They are cheering!

"Congratulations, Rapunzel! You've got the part," Mrs. Vargo smiles. "You must be new here. With that long hair, I know I'd remember you!"

THE END
TO FOLLOW ANOTHER PATH, TURN TO PAGE 9.

40

41

CHAPTER 3

RAPUNZEL THE GAMER

In the eyes of most teenagers, you have the perfect life — you are a professional gamer. Your name is Rae, but your gamer tag name is Rapunzel. Your avatar in the game highlights your best feature: your long, flowing hair. You play on Team Grimm, one of the highest-ranked teams in the world.

You started gaming for fun with your friends. Quickly you realized you were good — really good. Then, just like a fairy godmother, the manager of Team Grimm appeared. Manager Gothel said she wanted you to be on her team. You jumped at the chance.

Overall you think Ms. Gothel has done a fine job managing your team. She gets you into the best online tournaments. Your team has won most of them and received huge cash prizes. Most of that money has gone to what Ms. Gothel calls "business expenses." You haven't given much thought to it before. You just love to play.

What started as something fun to do with your friends has become a full-time job. Your parents are onion farmers, and money is tight. The money you earn playing makes a big difference. But as your team wins more tournaments, Ms. Gothel wants you to practice even more. She has even convinced your parents to let you live in a gaming room high up in her attic.

Ms. Gothel keeps the team's connection to the outside world limited. She says it's to keep everyone focused on the game.

Ms. Gothel provides all of the computer equipment, and the team plays on secure servers. The team communicates with her by video chat. No one is allowed to chat with the other teammates. "You aren't paid to socialize," she always says. "You're paid to win!"

Logging off after practice one day, you see a video chat request. You assume it is Ms. Gothel and click on it. You are shocked when a cute boy's face pops up on the screen instead.

"Rapunzel, it's Jack. I mean The Prince," he says. You only know your teammates by their gamer tag names.

45

TURN THE PAGE.

You can't hide your surprise. "Oh, hey! How

did you find me?"

"I did a little hacking into the video chat system," Jack says proudly.

"Oh," you reply. "Don't you think Ms. Gothel will be mad? She's pretty clear about us only talking during the game."

Jack shrugs. "Yeah, I guess so. I never understood why she doesn't want us to talk."

You don't understand it either, but the idea of going against Ms. Gothel's rules makes you nervous. You don't want to get kicked off the team.

Jack frowns. He seems nervous too. "Technically Ms. Gothel said we couldn't video chat with each other. How about we meet somewhere instead?"

47

TO SAY NO TO JACK'S INVITATION, TURN TO PAGE 48.

TO AGREE TO MEET JACK, TURN TO PAGE 51.

Your nerves get the better of you. "We'd better not," you tell Jack sadly.

"Oh," Jack says, frowning. "I understand."

After you say goodbye, you slump miserably in your chair. You wanted to meet Jack. It gets so lonely up in the attic with only Ms. Gothel to talk to.

As if she knew you were thinking of her, Ms. Gothel's face appears on your screen. "Rapunzel! Are you there?" she shrieks.

You sit up straight. "Yes, Ms. Gothel. I'm here. I just finished my practice."

"Your computer shows that you and The Prince were just video chatting, is that correct?" she demands.

"Um . . . well, yes," you tell her nervously, "but only for a minute."

Ms. Gothel's angry face fills your monitor. "Was I not clear about video chatting?" she asks harshly.

"I-I-I," you stammer. You've never seen her face quite this shade of angry red before.

"You are one of the highest-ranked gamers in the world because of me! I told you that winning takes dedication and focus, not socializing!" Ms. Gothel shouts.

"Yes, Ms. Gothel," you mumble.

"Now get back to practicing!" Ms. Gothel yells before disconnecting.

You are about to log back on to the game, when you hear someone knocking on the front door. You head downstairs and find Jack waiting outside.

"What are you doing here?" you ask, stunned.

"I need to show you something," Jack says. "Do you have a computer here besides your gaming equipment?"

50

"I have an old laptop from my parents," you tell him.

"OK, good. I need to borrow it," Jack says.

TURN TO PAGE 60.

What could it hurt to meet Jack? you think. You know Ms. Gothel will be mad if she finds out. You have to be careful. Jack gives you the address of a pizza place nearby. You pick a time to meet the next afternoon, and you both log off.

The next day you sneak quietly down the back stairway and out of the house, relieved that Ms. Gothel didn't see you. You are full of excitement as you walk along the sidewalk. You can't remember the last time you got out of that dark gaming room.

As you pass a newsstand, something catches your eye. A picture of your avatar, Rapunzel, is on the cover of *Gamer* magazine. You take the magazine off the shelf to get a closer look. The headline reads "World's Greatest Gamer Remains a Mystery." With shaking hands you flip to the article. It says that Rapunzel is one of the highest-ranked players in the world, but no one knows who she really is.

The article goes on to introduce Ms. Gothel as the face of Team Grimm. "The team has chosen to remain anonymous," Ms. Gothel is quoted as saying. "I represent them at all gaming events."

What is going on? you wonder. You buy the magazine and race to the pizza place. The article definitely has you rattled. As you walk you notice a man in a black suit on the other side of the street. He's looking at you intently. As you turn a corner, he crosses the street and heads the same way.

You see Jack as you enter the pizza place. You race over to tell him about the magazine. Before you can say a word, you see the man in the black suit enter the restaurant. He heads toward your table.

53

TO SEE WHAT THE MAN IN THE BLACK SUIT WANTS, TURN TO PAGE 54.

TO LEAVE THE RESTAURANT, TURN TO PAGE 67.

The man in the black suit stands at your table with a big smile on his face. He extends his hand.

"Hello! My name is Jacob Wilhelm of Team H.E.A.," he says. You recognize the team name right away. Team H.E.A. is your biggest competitor. "You must be Rapunzel."

"Rae," you correct him and shake his hand. How does he know who you are?

"You are a very hard person to track down, Rae," Mr. Wilhelm says. "I noticed you looking at *Gamer* magazine. When I saw your reaction to the cover, I knew you had to be Rapunzel."

You don't know what to say. You're so confused. Then you remember Jack is sitting at the table. "This is The Prince," you tell Mr. Wilhelm.

"It's a pleasure to meet you," he says, shaking Jack's hand. "This must be my lucky day! May I sit down and buy you each a slice? I have a business proposal for you."

55

TO LET MR. WILHELM JOIN YOU, TURN TO PAGE 56.

TO SAY NO, TURN TO PAGE 58.

You and Jack exchange looks. Jack shrugs his shoulders.

"OK, sure," you tell Mr. Wilhelm.

"Great," he says with a smile. "Here's the deal. I've been trying to speak to you two for some time, but I've never been able to get past Ms. Gothel. You are two of the best gamers out there. I'm putting together a new team, and I want you both as team captains. My plan is to showcase you and the rest of the team at the tournament in Hawaii next month."

"Hawaii?" you ask. "Ms. Gothel said all tournaments are played online."

Mr. Wilhelm shakes his head. "I always wondered why Team Grimm only played in the online tournaments. I'm guessing Ms. Gothel wanted to keep you all to herself."

Mr. Wilhelm continues. "Our team plays in tournaments all over the world. The players split the winnings, with a percentage for me of course."

You look at Jack. He looks back and says, "Why didn't we know this?"

"I'm not sure," you reply, overwhelmed by all you've heard. Could it really be true? You know Ms. Gothel is strict, but you've always assumed she had your best interest in mind. Could she really be using you for her own fame and fortune? It seems hard to believe. Maybe Mr. Wilhelm is making it all up so you leave Team Grimm.

57

"What do you say?" Mr. Wilhelm asks. "Do you two want to join Team H.E.A.?"

TO SAY NO, AND STAY ON TEAM GRIMM,
TURN TO PAGE 58.

TO SAY YES, AND JOIN TEAM H.E.A.,
TURN TO PAGE 69.

"I'm sorry, Mr. Wilhelm," you say. "My loyalty is to Team Grimm. Thanks, but no thanks."

Jack looks surprised, but he says, "I guess it's no for me too."

"I'm sorry to hear that," Mr. Wilhelm says as he hands you his business card. "You are both terrific players. Call me if you change your minds."

When Mr. Wilhelm is gone, Jack snaps his head toward you. "Why did you say no?"

"Because we need to figure out what is going on with Ms. Gothel and Team Grimm. I found this magazine on the way over," you explain as you show Jack the article.

Jack frowns as he reads. When he is finished, he asks, "Is there a computer at your house besides your Team Grimm equipment?"

"I have an old laptop from my parents," you tell him.

"Can I come over and borrow it?" Jack asks. "I want to do some investigating."

TO SAY YES, AND GO BACK TO MS. GOTHEL'S HOUSE,
TURN TO PAGE 60.

TO GET COLD FEET, AND SAY NO,
TURN TO PAGE 65.

You agree to let Jack use your laptop.

"Is Ms. Gothel home?" Jack asks cautiously. You remember Ms. Gothel said she had a meeting this afternoon.

"No, she's gone today," you say. You and Jack head inside the house and go up to your gaming room in the attic.

"Why don't you just use your Team Grimm computer?" you ask Jack as you set your laptop down in front of him.

"Ms. Gothel monitors our team computers. I don't want her to know what we're up to just yet," Jack replies.

You log onto the laptop, and Jack starts an Internet search. The screen fills with online articles about professional gaming.

You read over Jack's shoulder. You are shocked. There are tournaments being played all around the world. Gamers are treated like rock stars and are making huge amounts of money.

"Why would Ms. Gothel keep this from us?" you ask.

"So she can keep the fame and fortune for herself," Jack replies.

"What do we do now?" you wonder out loud.

"There's nothing you can do!" booms a voice from the doorway. You spin around to find Ms. Gothel glaring at both of you.

"Ms. Gothel!" you say with a start.

"You're wrong, Gothel," Jack tells her. "There is something we can do. We can leave Team Grimm."

"Oh, really?" Ms. Gothel says with a smirk as she holds up a piece of paper. "I thought you two might be up to something when I found you chatting. I just met with Rae's parents. They signed a 20-year contract for her to play on Team Grimm. They were happy to do it once I promised them another 1 percent of the profits. I'm off to meet your parents next, Jack!"

"That's not fair!" Jack says. "You'll never get away with this." Jack races toward Ms. Gothel and tries to grab the contract from her hand. She moves out of the way just in time, causing Jack to stumble and fall down the stairs. *Thump! Thump!* **63** *Thump! Crash!*

You hear Jack scream out in pain from the bottom of the steps. "My wrist! I think it's broken!"

"It sounds like he won't be gaming any time soon," Ms. Gothel says with a scowl. "It's a pity. He was one of my best players. I guess he should have listened."

Closing the door as she walks out of the attic, Ms. Gothel turns and says, "And you, Rapunzel, will be in this room for a long, long time!"

THE END

TO FOLLOW ANOTHER PATH, TURN TO PAGE 9.

Your head is spinning. You've always trusted Ms. Gothel. This can't be right. You wonder why you left your gaming room in the first place. At least up there everything made sense. Now you might lose it all.

"You can't come over, Jack," you say. "I live at Ms. Gothel's house. She'll see you, and we'll both be off the team." You let out a deep sigh. "I think we should just drop all of this. I'm going home. We have a game tonight."

Later that evening Team Grimm is in an online battle set in a land far, far away. You have climbed high up to the highest tower and are scoping out the enemy.

"Rapunzel, Rapunzel, let down your hair!" The Prince calls from below. You throw your avatar's long hair out of the window, and The Prince to starts to climb up.

You are about to give the order to attack, when The Prince suddenly loses his grip and falls into the sharp thorns below. You roll your eyes and wait for The Prince to reenter the game, but he never does.

"Come on, Jack. Hurry up!" you say impatiently to your computer. You can see the enemy approaching.

Suddenly a message appears on the bottom of your screen:
The Prince has been removed from Team Grimm. Let that teach you all a lesson about breaking my rules. Now get back to the game.

Signed, Ms. Gothel

66

THE END

TO FOLLOW ANOTHER PATH, TURN TO PAGE 9.

You jump up from the table. "On second thought there's an even better restaurant a few blocks away," you tell Jack. He looks confused but follows you toward the back door.

As soon as you sit down at the new restaurant, you try to explain. "I think that man was following me," you say, looking over your shoulder. "Do you think Ms. Gothel would send someone to spy on us?"

Jack looks at you like you're crazy. Then you pull out the magazine. "It's not as crazy as it sounds. Look at this magazine I found on my way over!"

Jack reads through the article with wide eyes. When he finishes reading, he slaps the table. "I knew it!" he exclaims.

"Knew what?" you ask, confused.

"Ms. Gothel controls our Internet access, right?" Jack asks.

"Yeah, to keep us focused on the game," you say.

"No, to keep us in the dark," Jack replies. "When we started winning tournaments, I thought we were getting big in the gaming world. This article confirms it. Team Grimm is a huge success, and Ms. Gothel is keeping all the fame — and money — for herself!"

You can't believe what you're hearing. You have been so grateful to Ms. Gothel, but she's been using you all along! "What should we do?" you ask.

68   Jack smiles. "Let's get in touch with the rest of Team Grimm. Cinderella and Rumpelstiltskin deserve to know what the wicked Ms. Gothel has been up to."

GO TO PAGE 69.

A month later you are on a beach in Hawaii. You and Jack both quit Team Grimm. You were even able to convince your new manager, Mr. Wilhelm, to recruit Cinderella and Rumpelstiltskin. The four of you have just won your first major tournament as Team H.E.A.

"Here's to the newest members of Team H.E.A.," Mr. Wilhelm says and raises up his coconut milkshake.

While you and the rest of the team sip your frosty treats, something occurs to you. "Mr. Wilhelm, I've been meaning to ask," you begin. "What does 'H.E.A.' stand for anyway?"

A smile crosses Mr. Wilhelm's face, and he says, "Happily ever after, of course!"

THE END

TO FOLLOW ANOTHER PATH, TURN TO PAGE 9.

CHAPTER 4

RAPUNZEL WAS A BRAT!

It all started with your garden and a bunch of rampions. You love your garden. You've worked very hard on it and it shows — you have the most beautiful flowers and the most delicious vegetables in town. You've even won a few awards in county fairs. You live a quiet life by yourself, and you prefer it that way. A large wall separates your small cottage from the rest of the town.

71

Lately it seems your garden may be a little too perfect. You think some of the kids in town have climbed your wall and snuck inside. Some of your flowers and veggies have gone missing.

One day as you tend to your crops, you hear a rustling from the other side of the garden.

The little thieves are back, you think. *I'm putting an end to this.*

You move quietly across the garden, determined to catch the kids red-handed. But when you reach the other side, you are shocked by what you see. It's your next-door neighbor! He is stealing your rampions. The delicate, edible flowers are being crushed in his meaty hands.

"Just what do you think you are doing?" you demand. You've never liked your neighbor. Now you know why.

"Dame Gothel!" he shrieks. "I-I was just . . ."

"You were stealing from me!" you shriek.

"I just wanted some of your rampions for my wife," he explains. "She's pregnant, you see, and she said she'll just die without them."

"*My* rampions? You mean the rampions I raised from baby seedlings? Covered on cold nights? Watered and fed to grow healthy and strong? Kept safe from hungry rabbits? Do you have any idea how much time and energy I've put into them? How about you give me your firstborn child, and we'll call it even?" you say sarcastically.

Without a word your neighbor snatches the rest of your rampions and heads up the wall. As he jumps over, he sneaks a peek back at you. You glare and point a finger menacingly at him. His eyes grow wide with fright as he falls over the side. You hope that will be enough to keep him out.

A few months later, there is a knock at your door. When you open it, you find your neighbor. He hands you a tiny baby girl. She looks no more than a few days old.

"For the rampions," he says and runs off.

You are shocked. Did this man really just give you his baby? Still holding the newborn, you march over to his house and pound on the door. No answer. You peek in a window and see that the whole place had been abandoned. There is no sign of your neighbor anywhere.

"It's probably for the best," you say to the sleeping baby in your arms. "What kind of parent trades his child for salad fixings anyway?"

You decide to name the girl Rapunzel. For years the two of you live a cozy life by yourselves inside the walls of your garden. From a young age, Rapunzel is blessed with beauty. She has the most magnificent hair.

It's so lovely, you think. *It would be a shame to cut it.* You let Rapunzel's hair grow and grow.

As the years go by, Rapunzel changes from a child into a young woman. And her mood changes as well. The sweet little girl has turned mean and unhappy. She gets annoyed at everything you say and do.

75

TURN THE PAGE.

Lately Rapunzel has been bugging you to take her to town. You prefer to keep to yourself and have been putting her off, but she won't drop it.

"I hate being stuck in this tiny cottage," Rapunzel complains. "There is nothing to do here!"

You wonder if a little space would help Rapunzel's mood. The two of you have been living together in your small cottage since she was born. Maybe she is ready for her own place. Would that be enough?

77

TO TAKE RAPUNZEL INTO TOWN, TURN TO PAGE 78.

TO BUILD RAPUNZEL A PLACE OF HER OWN, TURN TO PAGE 91.

"Please? Please, please, please can we go into town?" Rapunzel begs.

"I don't know," you say with a sigh. You worry the town is no place for Rapunzel. You've never told her why you've avoided the town all these years, and you'd like to keep it that way. But Rapunzel just won't stop.

"Oh, fine!" you say, finally giving in.

The next day you cover your head in a giant scarf. You don't want anyone to recognize you. But when you arrive in town, you realize there was no need to worry — no one is looking at you. All eyes are on Rapunzel. With her long, flowing hair, they look at her like she is the most beautiful girl they have ever seen. The two of you stroll through the market arm in arm.

You can tell Rapunzel doesn't like holding
on to you, but she loves the attention from the
townspeople. Maybe coming into town wasn't
such a bad idea. As you admire a vendor's fabric,
you notice a young man standing nearby. He is
smiling at Rapunzel. You see her blush as she
smiles back.

Coming into town is one thing, but mixing with the townspeople is another. You take Rapunzel's arm more firmly and steer her into a nearby café. As the two of you sit down to enjoy a cup of tea, the young man from the market approaches your table.

"Hello," he says. "I am the king's son." Rapunzel smiles broadly. You look around and notice that everyone in the café has stopped talking. They are all looking toward your table. You worry that your secret is about to be exposed.

80

"Excuse us," you say as you jump up to leave the café. The smile vanishes from Rapunzel's face, and she shoots you an awful look.

As you turn to leave, your scarf falls off your head. The townspeople gasp when they recognize you.

Rapunzel looks around the café. She turns back to you and asks, "What's going on?"

TO TELL RAPUNZEL NOTHING AND GO HOME,
TURN TO PAGE 82.

TO TELL RAPUNZEL YOUR SECRET,
TURN TO PAGE 84.

"It's nothing," you say quickly to Rapunzel. "You wanted to see the town and now you have. It's time to go!"

Rapunzel gets up in a huff and snaps at you, "Leave? We just got here! Why don't *you* leave? I love it here!"

"Rapunzel, you are coming home with me this instant!" you yell.

The whole way home, Rapunzel yells horrible things at you. "How could you embarrass me like that? You are the worst!"

By the time you are home, Rapunzel's mood has gone from bad to worse. "I can't stand you!" she screams at you. "I hate living with you. I never want to see you again!"

Rapunzel storms into her room and slams the door. You can hear her yelling and smashing things on the other side. Suddenly you have an idea. You race to the tool shed and bring back what you need.

"I think we both could use some space," you say as you install a bolt on the outside of her door to lock her inside. "You can stay in there until you change your attitude."

When you are finished, you walk to the kitchen and make yourself a cup of tea. You head out to your garden and enjoy the peace and quiet for the first time in a long time.

83

"That's better," you say to yourself as you sip your tea.

THE END

TO FOLLOW ANOTHER PATH, TURN TO PAGE 9.

You had hoped to keep your secret from Rapunzel, but maybe she's old enough to learn the truth.

"Will you give us a moment, please?" you say to the king's son.

"Sure," he replies. He looks confused. If he recognizes you, he isn't showing it.

You can tell Rapunzel is getting mad. "What is going on?" she snaps at you. "This is so embarrassing!"

You take a deep breath. "Long ago I lived in the heart of this town. I had the most beautiful garden in all the land. Everyone loved it. I had lots of friends who would come spend time with me there."

You take a deep breath. "One of my closest friends grew jealous of the attention I was getting. She started a rumor that I was a witch," you say in a soft voice. "The rumor spread and the townspeople became frightened of me. I was bullied and shunned by everyone. It was so terrible, I left town. I built my house and the high walls around it to be left alone."

A tear rolls down your cheek as you continue. "I didn't realize how lonely I was until you came into my life. But I can see that you don't belong closed off from the world with me in a small cottage. You should stay and enjoy your life."

85

You get up to leave the café. When you get to the door, Rapunzel calls out, "Wait!"

TO LEAVE THE CAFÉ,
TURN TO PAGE 86.

TO HEAR WHAT RAPUNZEL HAS TO SAY,
TURN TO PAGE 89.

Rapunzel has been so unhappy. You know she would be better off living in town. You leave the café and go home.

You spend your days alone again in your garden. Your flowers are still beautiful and your vegetables are still delicious, but they don't bring you the joy they once did. Rapunzel may have been difficult, but you find yourself missing her.

A few years later, there is a knock at your gate. When you open it, you are surprised to see Rapunzel. She is all grown up! She tells you that she has married the king's son. Together they have a son and a daughter.

"I wanted to come back and say thank you," Rapunzel says.

"You're thanking me?" you ask.

"Yes," she replies. "Thank you for bringing me to town that day. At first I was angry and lonely living by myself. Then I began to understand how you must have felt living out here on your own. Then I had my children. I realized how much you had done for me and what a horrible person I was to you."

87

TURN THE PAGE.

You are so pleased to see that Rapunzel has turned into such a wonderful adult. After that Rapunzel brings the children to visit often. They love to garden with Granny Gothel.

Rapunzel tells you that the rumor about you being a witch has been all but forgotten. She has told the townspeople how wonderful you are. Her friends from town bring their children to visit you too. One day you are showing a group of children how to harvest rampions.

"You are so good with children," one of Rapunzel's friends says. "You should open up a daycare. The whole town could bring their children over!"

You smile and shake your head. "No, I'm done raising the townspeople's children," you say.

THE END

TO FOLLOW ANOTHER PATH, TURN TO PAGE 9.

88

You stop at the door and turn around to face Rapunzel. She's smiling, but you can't quite read the look on her face.

You slowly make your way back to the table. You can feel everyone in the café watching you, but you don't care. You focus on Rapunzel. Is she finally going to apologize for her bad behavior? Maybe things can go back to the way they were when she was younger.

You sit down across from Rapunzel, and she takes your hand. You smile. Then Rapunzel starts to squeeze your hand a bit too hard.

Rapunzel leans closer and hisses in your ear, "You are totally embarrassing me in front of the king's son! Why do you have to ruin everything?"

90

You roll your eyes and sigh. *I should have just let my neighbor keep stealing those darn rampions,* you think.

THE END

TO FOLLOW ANOTHER PATH, TURN TO PAGE 9.

Rapunzel is getting older. She is ready for her own place. You secretly contact local builders. You ask them to build Rapunzel a room in an abandoned tower on your property.

When Rapunzel's new room is finished, you tell her to close her eyes as you walk across the lawn. "Ta-da!" you say.

Rapunzel opens her eyes. "It's a tower," she says with a look of disgust. "So what?"

"Yes, but I had a room built in it just for you," you tell her.

There is a rickety ladder propped against the side. A small sign from the builders is attached: *Use ladder to enter.*

Great, you think. *They said everything was ready, but the stairs aren't done.*

You've already told Rapunzel about her new place, so you climb up. You crawl through the window into a nice spacious room. There is a gorgeous view from the window.

As Rapunzel climbs into the window, her dress gets stuck on the ladder. Annoyed, she kicks the ladder. It falls and breaks into a million pieces on the ground.

"This is OK, I guess," Rapunzel says as she looks around the room. You see a hint of a smile for the first time in a long time. Then her smile is replaced with a frown. "Wait. Where's the door? How do we get out of here?"

You look around the room, wondering what she is talking about. Of course there is a door. There must be! When you don't see anything, your heart drops. The builders must have sealed over the door to the stairs when they were finishing the walls.

Why did I hire Grimm Brothers Construction in the first place? you think. *No wonder people say their work always ends in tragedy.*

You look for something to hang out the window and climb down. There are no curtains or sheets to tie together.

Rapunzel looks out the window and twirls her hair.

"If we jump out the window, we may be able to reach that tree branch and climb down," she suggests.

You look out the window at the tree. You wonder if you'll be able to make the jump safely at your age. Seeing Rapunzel twirl her long locks gives you another idea.

94

TO JUMP OUT THE WINDOW,
GO TO PAGE 95.

TO TELL RAPUNZEL YOUR IDEA,
TURN TO PAGE 97.

"Well? Are we jumping or not?" Rapunzel asks impatiently. "I'm not waiting." Before you can stop her, she leaps out the window. She almost misses the tree branch but is able to grab it at the last second.

"Geez, thanks for the room. What kind of genius hires builders who cover over the only door?" Rapunzel shouts sarcastically as she works her way down the tree. You hear her call out in pain as she reaches a thorny bush at the bottom. She calls up to you, "Now it's your turn. Let's see how you like climbing down a tree and landing in thorns!"

95

TURN THE PAGE.

You are certain you would not be able to make that jump and climb down the tree.

"I have a better idea," you call. "Why don't you go find a ladder or rope for me to use?"

"Seriously?" Rapunzel rolls her eyes. "You get us into this mess, and you expect me to help you?"

You glance around the room full of comfy furniture and bright light. Then you look out the window at the gorgeous view. The thought of some peace and quiet makes you smile.

"You're right," you yell to her. "I'll stay up here, and you can live in the cottage by yourself!

THE END

TO FOLLOW ANOTHER PATH, TURN TO PAGE 9.

"That's one idea," you tell Rapunzel, "but that tree is awfully far away. What if we hung your hair out the window? I could climb down and get a ladder."

Rapunzel looks at you as if you've gone mad. Then she looks again at the tree. With a sigh she says, "I guess we could try it."

Rapunzel dangles her hair out the window, and you test your weight. Her hair works perfectly! You are down the tower in no time. You start looking for a new ladder or some rope.

"Hurry up, down there," Rapunzel calls from above. "You are so slow and old!"

You realize right away how nice it is to have Rapunzel out of the house. What's the hurry getting her down? "That's right, I am slow and old," you yell back. "It may take a while to get you down!"

Thanks to Rapunzel's hair, you are able to visit and bring her food regularly.

"Rapunzel, Rapunzel, let down your hair!" you call up one afternoon. You've brought her some lunch along with her favorite cake.

You climb into the room and find Rapunzel is in an especially bad mood. As you eat she snaps, "You should take it easy on those desserts. You're getting too heavy, and it takes you so long to climb up. The king's son practically flies up!"

You can't believe your ears. The king's son has been here? You are furious! You have done so much for Rapunzel. You have given her a wonderful life after her parents abandoned her. You've put up with her terrible moods for years. And now she has the nerve to invite friends over? She didn't even ask your permission! You are about to ground her in this tower even longer when you hear a voice calling from below.

99

TURN THE PAGE.

"Rapunzel, Rapunzel, let down your hair!" It's the king's son.

Rapunzel smiles down at the king's son. She puts her hair out the window for him to climb. Then Rapunzel looks back at you, and a dark look crosses her face.

"Don't you ruin this for me, Witch!" she hisses at you.

You are shocked. "What did you call me?"

"You heard me! The king's son told me you're a witch," Rapunzel snaps. "Don't try to deny it. Everyone in town knows!"

100

TO KEEP THE KING'S SON FROM ENTERING THE TOWER,
GO TO PAGE 101.

TO CONFRONT THE KING'S SON,
TURN TO PAGE 103.

The king's son has been spreading awful rumors about you — rumors that you hoped had died long ago. Now he's turned Rapunzel against you. The pain and anger you've felt for years bubbles up to the surface. You are full of rage!

You see a pair a scissors on the desk. In a flash you grab them and lunge at Rapunzel. You begin to chop off her hair as fast as you can.

Rapunzel struggles and tries to pull away, but you keep cutting. After the last cut, you hear a loud crash. Outside the window you see the king's son land painfully in a bush of thorns below.

"My eyes!" he calls out in pain. "I'm blind!"

Rapunzel turns to you in shock. "What have you done? You really *are* a witch!"

"Rapunzel, you are about to find out what a witch I can be," you say. "I am sending you far, far away. You'll never see the king's son again!"

THE END

TO FOLLOW ANOTHER PATH, TURN TO PAGE 9.

You are fuming as the king's son enters through the window. He is holding a large bouquet of flowers.

"It's nice to meet you, Dame Gothel," he says, handing you the flowers. "Rapunzel has told me so much about you."

"Oh, really?" you reply sourly. "And just what have you been telling her? That I'm a witch?"

The king's son looks horrified. "No! I told Rapunzel that there was a *rumor* in town that you were a witch. After all the nice things she said about you, I knew it couldn't be true."

103

"Nice things?" you question. Maybe spending time with the king's son has improved Rapunzel's attitude.

TURN THE PAGE.

The king's son looks nervously at you. "I love Rapunzel, and I've come to ask you for her hand in marriage. We'll live together in the castle, but I promise we'll come see you often, and you are always welcome to visit."

"Well, yes," you say surprised. "You have my blessing, young man."

You climb down the tower first using the rope the king's son brought with him. As you reach the bottom, you notice bushes with sharp thorns growing against the tower. The thorns remind you of Rapunzel's prickly attitude. Both can be painful. You hope that the king's son doesn't get hurt by either one.

THE END

TO FOLLOW ANOTHER PATH, TURN TO PAGE 9.

CHAPTER 5

A MAIDEN IN THE TOWER

The tale of a maiden in the tower was created hundreds of years ago. But unlike many fairy tales, it wasn't based on a story told from generation to generation.

In 1637 Italian writer Giambattista Basile wrote a story called *Petrosinella*. In the story a young girl with that name is given to a witch after her mother is caught stealing parsley from the witch's garden. The witch locks Petrosinella in a tower and uses her hair to climb up. Petrosinella escapes with the help of a prince who hears her singing.

In Basile's story Petrosinella and the prince leave behind three magical acorns. They each turn into an obstacle to help stop the witch from chasing them.

Sixty years later the story was retold by Charlotte-Rose de Caumont de la Force in France. While living in a convent, she wrote *Persinette*. The story is similar to *Rapunzel*, which the Brothers Grimm published in 1812. In both stories a girl is raised by a sorceress after the girl's father is caught stealing from a garden. The girl is locked in a tower at age 12 until a prince hears her singing years later. The sorceress cuts off the girl's hair and sends her to live in the wilderness. The sorceress then tricks the prince into climbing up the cut hair before sending him crashing into the thorns below, blinding him.

The girl gives birth to twins in the wilderness and eventually finds the prince. Her tears heal the prince's eyes, and he can see again. The sorceress continues to torment the girl and her prince until their love for each other overcomes the sorceress.

The most recent version of this fairy tale is the Disney movie *Tangled*, which was released in 2010. In this version the witch uses Rapunzel's hair for its healing powers. The prince is replaced with a thief who begrudgingly helps Rapunzel in order to get back a stolen crown.

In each of these versions, the character of Rapunzel is portrayed as patient and determined. She never gives up, no matter how difficult the situation may be.

OTHER PATHS TO EXPLORE

1. This book offers three different versions of the classic fairy tale *Rapunzel*. Create your own story about Rapunzel. What would be the setting? How would the characters be different in your story?

2. In chapter 4 the story is told from the witch's point of view. Imagine the story was told by the king's son. How would the story change? How would it stay the same?

3. The story of Rapunzel was based on the tale *Petrosinella*. Reread the story of Petrosinella in chapter 5. How is this story different from the *Rapunzel* fairy tale you know?